This book is your gateway to the exciting world of web development. While it's geared towards both beginners and those with some coding experience, having a basic understanding of computers and how they operate will be beneficial as you embark on this journey.

What You'll Learn

- HTML Fundamentals: Master the core concepts of HTML, the language that structures every webpage on the internet.
- Essential Elements: Explore a wide range of HTML elements, from headings and paragraphs to images and links.
- Organizing Content: Learn to structure information effectively using lists, tables, and semantic elements.
- User Interaction: Create interactive webpages with forms, gathering user input and providing feedback.
- Multimedia Embedding: Enrich your webpages with dynamic content by embedding audio and video.
- Styling with CSS: Get a sneak peek into the world of web design with CSS, adding visual flair to your webpages.
- VS Code Tips and Tricks: Boost your productivity with helpful tips and tricks for using Visual Studio Code.

Why This Book?

- Clear and Concise: Complex concepts are explained in simple and easy-to-understand language.
- Hands-On Approach: Practical examples and exercises reinforce your learning and help you apply your knowledge.
- Step-by-Step Guidance: Follow a structured learning path that gradually builds your skills and confidence.
- Focus on Best Practices: Learn to write clean, efficient, and semantically correct HTML code.

Who Should Read This Book?

- Aspiring web developers with basic computer literacy.
- Students learning web development in a classroom setting.
- Anyone who wants to build their own website or understand how websites work.

Embark on Your Web Development Journey

Open this book, dive into the world of HTML, and unlock your potential to create amazing web experiences.

Table of Contents

Mastering Basic HTML Structure

Welcome to the exciting world of web development! This chapter will guide you through the fundamentals of HTML, the backbone of every webpage you see on the internet. By the end of this chapter, you'll be able to create your own simple webpages from scratch. Let's dive in!

Why HTML Structure Matters

HTML, or HyperText Markup Language, provides the structure and content of a webpage. Think of it as the skeleton of your website, providing the foundation upon which all the visual elements and interactive features are built. A well-structured HTML document is crucial for several reasons:

- **Accessibility for Browsers:** Browsers use HTML to understand and render the content of a webpage. A clear structure ensures that browsers can easily interpret your code and display it correctly to users.

- **Improved SEO:** Search engines rely on HTML to understand the content of your pages. Using proper headings, semantic elements, and descriptive attributes helps search engines index your site effectively.

- **Maintainability:** A well-organized HTML document is easier to read, understand, and modify, both for you and for other developers who might work on the code in the future.

Setting Up Your Workspace Before we start writing HTML, let's set up your coding environment. We'll be using Visual Studio Code (VS Code) throughout this book, a popular code editor with excellent features for web development. You can download it for free from the official website (https://code.visualstudio.com/).

While VS Code is our preferred choice, remember that you can use any text editor you like to write HTML. The fundamental concepts remain the same regardless of the tool you use. First create a new folder named "Learning HTML". Inside that folder create a new file named "index.html". When you installed the VS Code, it was integrated to your operating system, be it Windows or Mac. Now, right click on that file and you should see an option called "Open with VS Code". Click that and your file will open in VS Code. **Your First HTML Document**

Let's create a simple HTML document. Open VS Code and create a new file named index.html. Now, type the following code:

```html
<!DOCTYPE html>
<html lang="en">
  <head>
    <meta charset="UTF-8" />
    <title>My First Webpage</title>
  </head>

  <body>
    <h1>Hello, World!</h1>
    <p>This is my first paragraph.</p>
  </body>
</html>
```

Save the file in your preferred location, then double click on the file and open it in your web browser. **You can also do it inside the editor by installing extensions but for now we'll focus on understanding the concepts. At the end of the book, I'll include more advanced tips and tricks of VS Code that real developers use in development.** Now, you should see a webpage with the heading "Hello, World!" and a paragraph of text below it. Congratulations, you've just created your first webpage!

Hello, World!

This is my first paragraph.

Let's break down this code snippet:

HTML

```
<!DOCTYPE html>
<html lang="en">
<head>
    <meta charset="UTF-8">
    <title>My First Webpage</title>
</head>

<body>
    <h1>Hello, World! </h1>
    <p>This is my first paragraph. </p>
</body>
</html>
```

- **<!DOCTYPE html>:** This declaration defines the document type and version of HTML being used. In this case, it's HTML5.
- **<html lang="en">:** This tag represents the root of the HTML document. The lang attribute specifies the language of the content, here it's English.
- **<head>:** This section contains meta-information about the HTML document, such as the character set, title, and links to external resources like CSS stylesheets.
    - o **<meta charset="UTF-8">:** Specifies the character encoding for the document, ensuring proper display of various characters and symbols.
    - o **<title>My First Webpage</title>:** Sets the title that appears in the browser tab or window title bar.
- **<body>:** This section contains the visible content of the webpage, including headings, paragraphs, images, and links.

o **\<h1\>Hello, World!\</h1\>**: This is a level 1 heading, the largest heading size in HTML.

o **\<p\>This is my first paragraph.\</p\>**: This tag defines a paragraph of text.

Essential HTML Elements

HTML uses elements to structure content. Elements are represented by tags, which are keywords enclosed in angle brackets (e.g., \<h1\>). Most elements have an opening tag (e.g., \<h1\>) and a closing tag (e.g., \</h1\>), with the content placed between them.

Here are some common HTML elements you'll frequently use:

- **Headings:** \<h1\> to \<h6\> define headings of different levels, with \<h1\> being the largest and \<h6\> the smallest.

- **Paragraphs:** \<p\> defines a paragraph of text.

- **Links:** \<a\> creates hyperlinks to other webpages or resources. The href attribute specifies the URL of the link. For example: \<a href="https://www.example.com"\>Visit Example\</a\>.

- **Images:** \<img\> embeds an image in the webpage. The src attribute specifies the image file path, and the alt attribute provides alternative text for screen readers and in case the image fails to load. For example: \<img src="image.jpg" alt= 'A beautiful landscape"\>.

- **Lists:** HTML supports ordered lists (\<ol\>) and unordered lists (\<ul\>). List items are defined using the \<li\> tag.

- **Divisions:** \<div\> is a generic container element used to group other elements for styling or scripting purposes.

Common Mistakes to Avoid

As a beginner, you might encounter some common HTML errors. Here are a few to watch out for:

- **Forgetting Closing Tags:** Always remember to close your HTML tags. For example, a paragraph should be enclosed in both opening and closing tags: \<p\>This is a paragraph.\</p\>.

- **Misusing Elements:** Use elements for their intended purpose. For instance, don't use headings just to make text larger; use CSS for styling.

- **Incorrect Nesting:** Elements should be nested correctly. For example, a list item (<li>) should be placed inside a list (<ul> or <ol>).

- **Typos in Tags and Attributes:** Double-check your code for any typos in tag names or attribute names. HTML is case-insensitive, but it's good practice to use lowercase for consistency.

Practice Time!

Now that you have a basic understanding of HTML structure, it's time to put your knowledge into practice. Try creating a simple webpage with a heading, a few paragraphs, an image, and a link. Experiment with different elements and see how they affect the layout and content of your page.

Remember, the best way to learn is by doing! Don't be afraid to experiment and make mistakes. That's how you'll truly grasp the concepts and become comfortable with HTML.

Mission: Recreate a simple news article layout from a popular website.

Try doing the mission on your own first, it will help you solidify the concepts you just learned. If you get stuck you can always look for help from the solution.

Solution:

```html
index.html ×
C: > Users > Biswajit > Desktop > index.html > ...
1  <!DOCTYPE html>
2  <html>
3    <head>
4      <title>My News Article</title>
5    </head>
6    <body>
7      <h1>Breaking News!</h1>
8      <p>
9        This is a paragraph of news text. It contains important information about
10       current events.
11     </p>
12     <h2>Subheading</h2>
13     <p>Another paragraph with more details about the news story.</p>
14   </body>
15 </html>
16
```

The webpage should look like this:

Breaking News!

This is a paragraph of news text. It contains important information about current events.

Subheading

Another paragraph with more details about the news story.

This chapter has provided you with a solid foundation in basic HTML structure. In the upcoming chapters, we'll delve deeper into HTML elements, attributes, and styling with CSS. Get ready to build more complex and visually appealing webpages!

Organizing Information with HTML Lists

In the previous chapter, we learned about the basic structure of an HTML document and explored some essential elements. Now, let's delve into how to organize information effectively using HTML lists. Lists are incredibly useful for presenting data in a structured and easily digestible format. Whether you're creating a navigation menu, outlining steps in a tutorial, or simply presenting a collection of items, lists are your go-to tool.

Types of HTML Lists

HTML offers two main types of lists:

- **Unordered Lists (<ul>):** Used for listing items where the order doesn't matter. Each item is marked with a bullet point by default.
- **Ordered Lists (<ol>):** Used for listing items where the order is significant. Each item is marked with a number or letter by default.

Creating Unordered Lists

To create an unordered list, use the <ul> tag to enclose the list items. Each list item is defined using the <li> (list item) tag. Here's an example:

```
index.html ×

C: > Users > Biswajit > Desktop > index.html > html > body > ul > li
1    <!DOCTYPE html>
2    <html>
3      <head>
4        <title>Lists</title>
5      </head>
6      <body>
7        <ul>
8          <li>Apples</li>
9          <li>Bananas</li>
10         <li>Oranges</li>
11       </ul>
12     </body>
13   </html>
14
```

This code will render a bulleted list of fruits in your web browser.

```
← → C  ⓘ File  C:/Users/Biswajit/Desktop/index.html
```

- Apples
- Bananas
- Oranges

Creating Ordered Lists

For ordered lists, use the <ol> tag instead of <ul>. Here's how you can create a numbered list of steps:

```
index.html ×

C: > Users > Biswajit > Desktop > index.html > html
1    <!DOCTYPE html>
2  ∨ <html>
3  ∨   <head>
4        <title>Lists</title>
5      </head>
6  ∨   <body>
7  ∨     <ol>
8          <li>Preheat the oven to 350°F (175°C).</li>
9          <li>Mix flour, sugar, and eggs in a bowl.</li>
10         <li>Pour the batter into a baking pan.</li>
11         <li>Bake for 30 minutes.</li>
12       </ol>
13     </body>
14 </html>
15
```

This will display a numbered list of baking instructions.

```
← → C  ⓘ File  C:/Users/Biswajit/Desktop/index.html
```

1. Preheat the oven to 350°F (175°C).
2. Mix flour, sugar, and eggs in a bowl.
3. Pour the batter into a baking pan.
4. Bake for 30 minutes.

This will display a numbered list of baking instructions.

Nesting Lists

You can create nested lists by placing a list inside another list item. This is useful for creating hierarchical structures or outlines. For example:

```html
<!DOCTYPE html>
<html>
  <head>
    <title>Lists</title>
  </head>
  <body>
    <ul>
      <li>
        Fruits
        <ul>
          <li>Apples</li>
          <li>Bananas</li>
        </ul>
      </li>
      <li>
        Vegetables
        <ul>
          <li>Carrots</li>
          <li>Spinach</li>
        </ul>
      </li>
    </ul>
  </body>
</html>
```

This code will create a nested list where "Fruits" and "Vegetables" are the main list items, each with its own sub-list of items.

- Fruits
  - Apples
  - Bananas
- Vegetables
  - Carrots
  - Spinach

Customizing List Styles

While the default bullet points and numbers are sufficient in many cases, HTML offers attributes and CSS properties for customizing the appearance of your lists. You can change the bullet style, numbering type, and indentation. We'll cover list styling in more detail in the CSS chapters.

Semantic Meaning of Lists

Remember to use lists not just for visual presentation but also to convey the semantic meaning of your content. If you're presenting a set of related items where order doesn't matter, use an unordered list. If the order is significant, use an ordered list. This helps improve the accessibility and SEO of your webpages.

Practical Applications

Lists are incredibly versatile and can be used in various scenarios:

- **Navigation Menus:** Create a list of links to different pages on your website.
- **Product Features:** List the key features of a product in an unordered or ordered list.
- **Tables of Contents:** Structure the sections of a document using nested lists.
- **Step-by-Step Instructions:** Present a sequence of steps in an ordered list.

By mastering the use of HTML lists, you can organize information effectively and enhance the user experience on your webpages. Remember to choose the appropriate list type, structure your content logically, and consider the semantic meaning of your lists.

Mission: Build a "Top 10" list of their favourite things.

Solution:

```
<!DOCTYPE html>
<html>
  <head>
    <title>My Top 10</title>
  </head>
  <body>
    <h1>My Top 10 Favorite Things</h1>
    <ol>
      <li>Pizza</li>
      <li>Coding</li>
      <li>Reading</li>
      <li>Hiking</li>
      <li>Music</li>
      <li>Movies</li>
      <li>Traveling</li>
      <li>Coffee</li>
      <li>Friends</li>
      <li>Family</li>
    </ol>
  </body>
</html>
```

Webpage:

My Top 10 Favorite Things

1. Pizza
2. Coding
3. Reading
4. Hiking
5. Music
6. Movies
7. Traveling
8. Coffee
9. Friends
10. Family

Embedding and Manipulating Images

Images are essential for creating engaging and visually appealing webpages. They can convey information, evoke emotions, and enhance the overall user experience. In this chapter, we'll explore how to embed images in your HTML documents and manipulate their appearance using various attributes and techniques.

The <img> Tag

The key to adding images to your webpages is the <img> tag. This tag is an empty element, meaning it doesn't have a closing tag. Instead, all the information about the image is provided within the tag's attributes.

Essential Attributes

- src (source): This attribute specifies the URL or file path of the image you want to embed. It's the most crucial attribute of the <img> tag, as it tells the browser where to find the image.

- alt (alternative text): This attribute provides a text description of the image. It's essential for accessibility, as it allows screen readers to convey the image's content to visually impaired users. It also serves as a fallback if the image cannot be displayed for any reason.

Here's an example of how to use the <img> tag:

```
index.html ×
C: > Users > Biswajit > Desktop > 🔲 index.html > ⬡ html > ⬡ body > ⬡ img
1    <!DOCTYPE html>
2    <html>
3      <head>
4        <title>Images</title>
5      </head>
6      <body>
7        <img src="images/my-image.jpg" alt="A beautiful sunset">
8      </body>
9    </html>
10
```

This code will embed an image named "my-image.jpg" located in the "images" folder. The alternative text "A beautiful sunset" will be displayed if the image cannot be loaded.

Image Formats

The web supports various image formats, each with its own strengths and weaknesses. Some common formats include:

- JPEG (Joint Photographic Experts Group): Suitable for photographs and images with complex colors and details.
- PNG (Portable Network Graphics): Supports transparency and is ideal for graphics, logos, and images with sharp lines.
- GIF (Graphics Interchange Format): Supports simple animations and is often used for small icons and animated images.

Choose the appropriate image format based on the type of image and its intended use.

Image Dimensions

You can control the size of an image using the width and height attributes. These attributes specify the width and height of the image in pixels.

```
index.html ×
C: > Users > Biswajit > Desktop > index.html > html
1   <!DOCTYPE html>
2   <html>
3     <head>
4       <title>Images</title>
5     </head>
6     <body>
7       <img src="https://encrypted-tbn0.gstatic.com/images?q=tbn:ANd9GcS-C_UAhXq96fuGO45ZEEzfbKnh1viQB9EDBQ&s" alt="A beautiful sunset" width="300"
        height="200">
8     </body>
9   </html>
10
```

This code will display the image with a width of 300 pixels and a height of 200 pixels.

Responsive Images

For a better user experience across different devices, it's crucial to make your images responsive. This means that the images should adjust their size and position based on the screen size and orientation of the device.

You can achieve responsiveness using CSS media queries and the max-width property. We'll cover responsive images in more detail in the CSS chapters.

Image Optimization

Optimizing images is crucial for website performance. Large image files can slow down page load times, leading to a poor user experience.

Here are some tips for optimizing images:

Choose the appropriate format: Use JPEG for photographs and PNG for graphics.

Compress images: Use image compression tools to reduce file size without significant loss of quality.

Resize images: Resize images to the dimensions they will be displayed on the webpage.

Use lazy loading: Load images only when they are visible in the viewport.

By following these optimization techniques, you can ensure that your images load quickly and efficiently, contributing to a positive user experience.

Accessibility Considerations

Always provide meaningful alternative text for your images using the alt attribute. This ensures that users with visual impairments can understand the content of the images.

Avoid using images as the sole source of crucial information. If an image conveys essential content, provide the same information in text form as well.

Practice Time!

Experiment with embedding different types of images in your webpages. Try adjusting their dimensions, using different formats, and writing descriptive alternative text. As you become more comfortable with the <img> tag and its attributes, you'll be able to create visually rich and accessible webpages that engage your users.

Mission: Create a mock "product page" for an imaginary invention.

Solution:

```
index.html ×
C: > Users > Biswajit > Desktop > index.html > html > body > p
1    <!DOCTYPE html>
2    <html>
3      <head>
4        <title>The Amazing Widget</title>
5      </head>
6      <body>
7        <h1>The Amazing Widget</h1>
8        <img src="widget.jpg" alt="A photo of the amazing widget" />
9        <p>
10           This is the most amazing widget you'll ever see! It does everything you
11           could ever want and more.
12       </p>
13     </body>
14   </html>
15
```

Webpage:

The Amazing Widget

This is the most amazing widget you'll ever see! It does everything you could ever want and more.

Structuring Data with HTML Tables

While lists are excellent for organizing sequential data, tables provide a powerful way to structure information in a grid format, making it easy to read and compare. Think of spreadsheets, timetables, or product catalogues – these are all examples of data best presented in tables. This chapter will guide you through the essentials of creating and customizing tables in HTML.

The <table> Element

The foundation of any HTML table is the <table> element. This tag signifies the beginning of your table and encapsulates all the rows and cells within it.

Rows and Cells

- <tr> (table row): Each row in your table is defined by the <tr> tag. You can have as many rows as needed to present your data.

- <td> (table data): Within each row, you use <td> tags to create individual cells. Each cell holds a single piece of data.

Let's create a simple table to illustrate this:

```
index.html  X
C: > Users > Biswajit > Desktop > index.html > html > body > table > tr > td
 1    <!DOCTYPE html>
 2    <html>
 3      <head>
 4        <title>Tables</title>
 5      </head>
 6      <body>
 7        <table>
 8          <tr>
 9            <td>Name</td>
10            <td>Age</td>
11            <td>City</td>
12          </tr>
13          <tr>
14            <td>John Doe</td>
15            <td>30</td>
16            <td>New York</td>
17          </tr>
18        </table>
19      </body>
20    </html>
21
```

This code will render a table with two rows and three columns. The first row acts as a header, while the second row contains data for a person.

Name   Age City
John Doe 30   New York

Table Headers

To make your tables more readable, you can use <th> (table header) elements instead of <td> for the header row. This will typically display the header text in bold and centre it within the cell.

```html
index.html ×

C: > Users > Biswajit > Desktop > index.html > html > body > table
1    <!DOCTYPE html>
2    <html>
3      <head>
4        <title>Tables</title>
5      </head>
6      <body>
7        <table>
8            <tr>
9               <th>Name</th>
10              <th>Age</th>
11              <th>City</th>
12           </tr>
13           <tr>
14              <td>John Doe</td>
15              <td>30</td>
16              <td>New York</td>
17           </tr>
18        </table>
19      </body>
20    </html>
21
```

Name Age City
John Doe 30 New York

Spanning Rows and Columns

Sometimes, you need to make a cell span across multiple rows or columns. This is where the rowspan and colspan attributes come in handy.

- **rowspan:** Specifies the number of rows a cell should span.

- **colspan:** Specifies the number of columns a cell should span.

Here's an example:

```
index.html ×
C: > Users > Biswajit > Desktop > index.html > html > body > table
1    <!DOCTYPE html>
2    <html>
3      <head>
4        <title>Tables</title>
5      </head>
6      <body>
7        <table>
8            <tr>
9              <th colspan="2">Contact Information</th>
10           </tr>
11           <tr>
12             <td>Email:</td>
13             <td>john.doe@example.com</td>
14           </tr>
15           <tr>
16             <td>Phone:</td>
17             <td>555-123-4567</td>
18           </tr>
19        </table>
20     </body>
21   </html>
22
```

In this code, the "Contact Information" header spans across two columns.

Contact Information

Email: john.doe@example.com

Phone: 555-123-4567

Table Captions

You can add a caption to your table using the <caption> element. This provides a concise description of the table's content.

```
index.html ×

C: > Users > Biswajit > Desktop > 🔲 index.html > ⊘ html > ⊘ body > ⊘ table
1    <!DOCTYPE html>
2    <html>
3      <head>
4        <title>Tables</title>
5      </head>
6      <body>
7        <table>
8            <caption>Employee Details</caption>
9            <tr>
10               <th>Name</th>
11               <th>Age</th>
12               <th>City</th>
13           </tr>
14           <tr>
15               <td>John Doe</td>
16               <td>30</td>
17               <td>New York</td>
18           </tr>
19         </table>
20       </body>
21   </html>
22
```

Employee Details

Name   Age   City

John Doe 30   New York

Accessibility Considerations

When creating tables, keep accessibility in mind:

- Use table headers (<th>) to clearly identify the purpose of each column.
- Use the scope attribute on header cells to explicitly associate them with their corresponding rows or columns.
- Keep your table structure simple and avoid overly complex layouts.
- Provide a summary of the table's content for screen readers if needed.

Advanced Table Features

HTML offers additional elements and attributes for more complex table structures, such as:

- **<thead>, <tbody>, <tfoot>:** These elements allow you to group rows into table header, body, and footer sections.
- **Nested tables:** You can embed tables within other tables for more intricate layouts.

We'll explore these advanced features in later chapters.

Practice Time!

Start creating tables to represent different types of data. Experiment with rows, columns, headers, and spanning cells. Remember to consider accessibility and semantic meaning as you structure your tables. With practice, you'll be able to create well-organized and informative tables that enhance your webpages.

Mission: Replicate a simple data table from a website.

Solution:

```html
1   <!DOCTYPE html>
2   <html>
3   <head>
4     <title>My Data Table</title>
5   </head>
6   <body>
7     <table>
8       <caption>My Favorite Books</caption>
9       <tr>
10        <th>Title</th>
11        <th>Author</th>
12      </tr>
13      <tr>
14        <td>The Hitchhiker's Guide to the Galaxy</td>
15        <td>Douglas Adams</td>
16      </tr>
17      <tr>
18        <td>Pride and Prejudice</td>
19        <td>Jane Austen</td>
20      </tr>
21    </table>
22  </body>
23  </html>
```

Webpage:

C:/Users/Biswajit/Desktop/index.html

My Favorite Books

Title	Author
The Hitchhiker's Guide to the Galaxy	Douglas Adams
Pride and Prejudice	Jane Austen

Forms: Gathering User Input

Websites are more than just static displays of information. They often need to interact with users, gathering data and responding to their actions. This is where HTML forms come into play. Forms provide a structured way to collect user input, enabling functionalities like user logins, contact forms, surveys, and online shopping. This chapter will guide you through the essentials of creating and using forms in your webpages.

The <form> Element

The <form> element is the cornerstone of user input in HTML. It acts as a container for various form controls, such as text fields, buttons, and checkboxes. All the input elements within a <form> tag are submitted together as a single unit.

Here's a basic example:

```
1  <!DOCTYPE html>
2  <html>
3  <head>
4    <title>Forms</title>
5  </head>
6  <body>
7    <form>
8        <label for="name">Name:</label>
9        <input type="text" id="name" name="name"><br><br>
10       <input type="submit" value="Submit">
11   </form>
12 </body>
13 </html>
```

This code creates a simple form with a text field for the user's name and a submit button.

Name: [   ]

[Submit]

Form Controls

HTML provides a variety of form controls to cater to different input types:

- **Text Fields (<input type="text">):** Allow users to enter single-line text input, such as their name or email address.
- **Password Fields (<input type="password">):** Similar to text fields, but mask the input for security purposes.
- **Radio Buttons (<input type="radio">):** Allow users to select one option from a group of choices.
- **Checkboxes (<input type="checkbox">):** Allow users to select multiple options from a set of choices.
- **Submit Buttons (<input type="submit">):** Trigger the form submission, sending the collected data to the server.
- **Text Areas (<textarea>):** Allow users to enter multi-line text, such as comments or feedback.
- **Select Lists (<select>):** Provide a dropdown list of options for users to choose from.

Labels and Input Associations

To improve usability and accessibility, it's essential to associate labels with their corresponding input fields. This helps users understand what information is required in each field.

The <label> element is used to create labels. You can associate a label with an input field by using the for attribute in the <label> and the id attribute in the input field.

```
index.html ×
C: > Users > Biswajit > Desktop > 🔲 index.html > ...
1    <!DOCTYPE html>
2    <html>
3      <head>
4        <title>Forms</title>
5      </head>
6      <body>
7        <form>
8          <label for="email">Email:</label>
9          <input type="email" id="email" name="email" />
10       </form>
11     </body>
12   </html>
13
```

Email: [   ]

Form Attributes

The <form> element has several attributes that control its behavior:

- **action:** Specifies the URL where the form data will be submitted.
- **method:** Specifies the HTTP method used for submission (usually "GET" or "POST").
- **enctype:** Specifies how the form data should be encoded before submission.

Form Validation

Form validation is crucial to ensure that users provide the required information in the correct format. You can use client-side validation (using JavaScript) or server-side validation (using a server-side language like PHP or Python) to validate form data.

Handling Form Data

Once a form is submitted, the data is sent to the server for processing. Server-side scripts can then use this data to perform various actions, such as storing it in a database, sending an email, or generating a response.

Practice Time!

Experiment with different form controls and attributes. Create forms for various purposes, such as contact forms, surveys, or login pages. Implement basic validation to ensure data integrity. As you gain more experience, you'll be able to create interactive and user-friendly forms that enhance your web applications.

Mission: Design a basic "survey form."

Solution:

Webpage:

← → C ⓘ File C:/Users/Biswajit/Desktop/index.html

My Survey

Name: [   ]

Email: [   ]

[Submit]

Hyperlinks: Connecting the Web with Links

The true power of the World Wide Web lies in its interconnectedness. Hyperlinks, or simply links, are the threads that weave this intricate web, allowing users to navigate seamlessly between different pages and resources. In this chapter, we'll explore the <a> (anchor) element, the gateway to creating hyperlinks in HTML.

The <a> Element and the href Attribute

The <a> element is used to create hyperlinks. The destination of the link is specified using the href (hypertext reference) attribute. This attribute can point to various resources:

- Other webpages: Link to other pages within your website or external websites.
- Files: Link to downloadable files like PDFs, documents, or images.
- Email addresses: Create links that open the user's email client with a pre-filled address.
- Specific sections within a page: Link to different sections of the same page using ID attributes.

Here's a basic example of linking to another webpage:

```
index.html  ×

C: > Users > Biswajit > Desktop > index.html > html
1   <!DOCTYPE html>
2   <html>
3   <head>
4       <title>Links</title>
5   </head>
6   <body>
7       <a href="https://www.example.com">Visit Example</a>
8   </body>
9   </html>
```

This code will create a hyperlink with the text "Visit Example" that, when clicked, takes the user to the website "www.example.com".

Visit Example

Link Targets

The target attribute specifies where the linked document should be opened. Here are the common values:

- **_blank:** Opens the link in a new browser tab or window.

- **_self:** Opens the link in the same frame or window as it was clicked (this is the default).

- **_parent:** Opens the link in the parent frame.

- **_top:** Opens the link in the full body of the window.

For instance, to open a link in a new tab:

```
1   <!DOCTYPE html>
2   <html>
3   <head>
4     <title>Links</title>
5   </head>
6   <body>
7       <a href="https://www.example.com" target="_blank">Visit Example in a new tab</a>
8   </body>
9   </html>
```

Link Text and Accessibility

The text between the opening and closing <a> tags is called the link text. This text should be descriptive and informative, clearly indicating the destination or purpose of the link. Avoid generic phrases like "click here" or "read more."

For accessibility, it's crucial to use link text that makes sense out of context. Screen reader users often navigate through a list of links, so each link's purpose should be clear from its text alone.

Email Links

To create a link that opens the user's email client:

```
index.html  ✕

C: > Users > Biswajit > Desktop > index.html > html
  1   <!DOCTYPE html>
  2   <html>
  3   <head>
  4     <title>Links</title>
  5   </head>
  6   <body>
  7       <a href="mailto:someone@example.com">Send Email</a>
  8   </body>
  9   </html>
```

This will create a link that, when clicked, opens a new email message addressed to "someone@example.com".

Send Email

Linking Within a Page

You can link to specific sections within the same page using ID attributes. First, assign a unique ID to the target element:

```
index.html  ✕

C: > Users > Biswajit > Desktop > index.html > html > body > h2#section2
  1   <!DOCTYPE html>
  2   <html>
  3   <head>
  4     <title>Links</title>
  5   </head>
  6   <body>
  7       <h2 id="section2">Section 2</h2>
  8   </body>
  9   </html>
```

Then, create a link to that ID using the href attribute with a hash (#) symbol followed by the ID:

```
index.html ×

C: > Users > Biswajit > Desktop > index.html > html > body
1    <!DOCTYPE html>
2    <html>
3    <head>
4      <title>Links</title>
5    </head>
6    <body>
7        <h2 id="section2">Section 2</h2>
8        <a href="#section2">Go to Section 2</a>
9    </body>
10   </html>
```

Styling Links

Links can be styled using CSS to change their color, font, and other visual properties. This allows you to create visually appealing and consistent links throughout your website.

Practice Time!

Experiment with creating different types of hyperlinks. Link to external websites, internal pages, files, and email addresses. Practice writing descriptive and accessible link text. As you gain more experience, you'll be able to use hyperlinks effectively to create a seamless and engaging user experience on your website.

Mission: Create a webpage with a collection of their favourite website links, categorized and organized.

Solution:

```
index.html ×

C: > Users > Biswajit > Desktop > index.html > html
1    <!DOCTYPE html>
2    <html>
3    <head>
4      <title>My Favorite Links</title>
5    </head>
6    <body>
7        <h1>My Favorite Links</h1>
8        <h2>News</h2>
9        <ul>
10           <li><a href="https://www.example-news-site.com">Example News Site</a></li>
11           <li><a href="https://www.another-news-site.com">Another News Site</a></li>
12       </ul>
13       <h2>Entertainment</h2>
14       <ul>
15           <li><a href="https://www.example-entertainment-site.com">Example Entertainment Site</a></li>
16       </ul>
17   </body>
18   </html>
```

Webpage:

My Favorite Links

News

- Example News Site
- Another News Site

Entertainment

- Example Entertainment Site

Multimedia: Embedding Audio and Video

In today's digital landscape, webpages are no longer limited to text and images. Multimedia elements like audio and video have become integral parts of the online experience, enriching websites with dynamic content and interactive features. This chapter will guide you through the process of embedding audio and video content in your HTML documents.

The <audio> Element

The <audio> element allows you to embed audio files directly into your webpages. Here's the basic syntax:

```
index.html  ×

C: > Users > Biswajit > Desktop > index.html > html > body > audio > source
1   <!DOCTYPE html>
2   <html>
3     <head>
4       <title>Multimedia</title>
5     </head>
6   <body>
7     <audio controls>
8       <source src="audio.mp3" type="audio/mpeg" />
9     </audio>
10  </body>
11  </html>
12
```

- **controls attribute: This attribute provides default playback controls like play, pause, volume, and timeline.**
- **<source> element: Specifies the audio file source. You can include multiple <source> elements to provide different file formats for compatibility with various browsers.**
- **Fallback content: The text between the <audio> tags will be displayed if the browser doesn't support the audio element.**

Supported Audio Formats

Different browsers support different audio formats. It's recommended to include multiple source files in different formats to ensure compatibility:

- **MP3:** Widely supported format with good compression.
- **WAV:** Uncompressed format with high quality but larger file size.
- **OGG:** Open-source format with good quality and compression.

The <video> Element

Similar to audio, the <video> element allows you to embed video content. Here's the basic syntax:

```html
<!DOCTYPE html>
<html>
  <head>
    <title>Multimedia</title>
  </head>
  <body>
    <video width="640" height="360" controls>
      <source src="video.mp4" type="video/mp4">
    </video>
  </body>
</html>
```

- **width and height attributes:** Specify the dimensions of the video player.
- **controls attribute:** Provides default video playback controls.
- **<source> element:** Specifies the video file source. Include multiple sources for different formats.
- **Fallback content:** Text displayed if the browser doesn't support the video element.

Supported Video Formats

Similar to audio, it's crucial to provide video files in multiple formats for compatibility:

- MP4: Widely supported format with good compression and quality.

- WebM: Open-source format with good compression and quality.

- Ogg: Another open-source format option.

Additional Attributes

Both <audio> and <video> elements support several other attributes for customization:

- autoplay: Starts playing the media automatically when the page loads.

- loop: Loops the media playback.

- muted: Mutes the audio by default.

- poster: Specifies an image to be displayed before the video starts playing.

Accessibility Considerations

- Captions and Subtitles: Provide captions and subtitles for your videos to make them accessible to users with hearing impairments. You can use the <track> element for this purpose.

- Transcripts: Offer transcripts of audio and video content for users who prefer to read or who cannot access the media.

- Alternative Text: Provide alternative text descriptions for any visual elements within the media player.

Practice Time!

Experiment with embedding different audio and video files in your webpages. Explore various attributes and customization options. Remember to prioritize accessibility by providing captions, subtitles, and transcripts whenever possible. By effectively incorporating multimedia, you can create engaging and informative web experiences.

Mission: Build a page featuring their favourite song or a short video clip with basic playback controls.

Try running this on your own with your own videos.

Solution:

Semantics: Structuring Content with Meaning

In the early days of the web, HTML was primarily used to define the visual presentation of documents. However, as the web evolved, so did the need for structure that conveyed meaning, not just appearance. This is where semantic HTML comes in. By using elements that accurately describe the content they contain, we create webpages that are more accessible, maintainable, and SEO-friendly. This chapter explores the importance of semantic HTML and introduces some of the key elements that bring meaning to your webpages.

What is Semantic HTML?

Semantic HTML involves using HTML elements to structure content based on its meaning, not just its visual appearance. Instead of relying solely on elements like <div> and <span> for generic layout, semantic HTML utilizes elements like <article>, <aside>, <nav>, and <footer> to describe the specific role of content within a webpage.

Benefits of Semantic HTML

- Accessibility: Screen readers and other assistive technologies rely on semantic HTML to understand the structure and content of a webpage, making it accessible to users with disabilities.

- SEO: Search engines use semantic HTML to understand the context and relevance of your content, improving your website's search engine rankings.

- Maintainability: Semantic HTML makes your code more organized and easier to understand, facilitating maintenance and updates.

- Interoperability: Semantic HTML ensures consistent rendering of your webpages across different browsers and devices.

Key Semantic HTML Elements

Here are some essential semantic HTML elements and their purposes:

- <article>: Represents a self-contained piece of content, such as a blog post, news article, or forum post.
- <aside>: Contains content that is tangentially related to the main content, such as sidebars, callouts, or advertisements.
- <nav>: Defines a section of navigation links.

- <header>: Represents the introductory content of a page or section.
- <footer>: Contains closing content, such as copyright information, contact details, or related links.
- <figure> and <figcaption>: Used to mark up figures and their captions.
- <main>: Specifies the main content of the document.
- <section>: Defines a thematic grouping of content within a page.

Example of Semantic HTML

Consider a blog post. Instead of using generic <div> elements to structure the layout, you can use semantic elements like this:

```html
<!DOCTYPE html>
<html>
  <head>
    <title>Sematics</title>
  </head>
  <body>
    <article>
      <header>
        <h1>Blog Post Title</h1>
        <p>Published on <time datetime="2024-11-28">November 28, 2024</time></p>
      </header>
      <main>
        <p>This is the main content of the blog post.</p>
      </main>
      <aside>
        <h3>About the Author</h3>
        <p>...</p>
      </aside>
      <footer>
        <p>&copy; 2024 Example Blog</p>
      </footer>
    </article>
  </body>
</html>
```

C:/Users/Biswajit/Desktop/index.html

Blog Post Title

Published on November 28, 2024

This is the main content of the blog post.

About the Author

...

© 2024 Example Blog

Choosing the Right Elements

Selecting the most appropriate semantic element depends on the specific context and purpose of your content. Carefully consider the meaning and role of each section within your webpage to choose the element that best represents it.

Practice Time!

Analyze existing webpages and identify opportunities to replace generic elements with semantic alternatives. Practice structuring your own webpages using semantic HTML. As you become more familiar with these elements, you'll be able to create websites that are not only visually appealing but also semantically rich and accessible to all users.

Mission: Redesign a previous mission's webpage using semantic HTML5 tags to improve its structure and accessibility.

Solution:

```html
<!DOCTYPE html>
<html>
<head>
    <title>My News Article</title>
</head>
<body>
    <article>
        <h1>Breaking News!</h1>
        <p>This is a paragraph of news text. It contains important information about current events.</p>
        <h2>Subheading</h2>
        <p>Another paragraph with more details about the news story.</p>
    </article>
</body>
</html>
```

Webpage:

Breaking News!

This is a paragraph of news text. It contains important information about current events.

Subheading

Another paragraph with more details about the news story.

Styling with CSS: A Sneak Peek into Web Design

While HTML provides the structure and content of a webpage, CSS (Cascading Style Sheets) brings it to life with visual flair. CSS allows you to control the presentation of your webpages, dictating everything from colors and fonts to layout and responsiveness. This chapter offers a glimpse into the world of web design with CSS, empowering you to transform your plain HTML documents into visually engaging and stylish webpages.

What is CSS?

CSS is a style sheet language used to describe the presentation of HTML documents. It allows you to separate the content from the presentation, making your code cleaner, more maintainable, and easier to update.

How to Apply CSS

There are three main ways to apply CSS to your HTML:

- Inline Styles: CSS rules are applied directly to an HTML element using the style attribute.
- Internal Stylesheet: CSS rules are defined within the <style> tag in the <head> section of the HTML document.
- External Stylesheet: CSS rules are written in a separate .css file and linked to the HTML document using the <link> tag.

Basic CSS Syntax

A CSS rule consists of a selector and a declaration block.

- Selector: Specifies the HTML element(s) to which the style will be applied.

- Declaration block: Contains one or more declarations, each consisting of a property and a value.

Here's an example:

```
1    p {
2        color: blue;
3        font-size: 16px;
4    }A
```

This CSS rule selects all <p> (paragraph) elements and sets their text color to blue and font size to 16 pixels.

Common CSS Properties

CSS offers a vast array of properties to style various aspects of your webpages. Here are some commonly used properties:

- **color:** Sets the text color.

- **font-size:** Specifies the font size.

- **font-family:** Defines the font to be used.

- **background-color:** Sets the background color of an element.

- **width and height:** Specify the dimensions of an element.

- **margin and padding:** Control the spacing around an element.

- **border:** Adds a border around an element.

The Box Model

The CSS box model is a fundamental concept that describes how elements are rendered on a webpage. Each element is represented as a rectangular box with content, padding, border, and margin. Understanding the box model is crucial for controlling the layout and spacing of your elements.

CSS Selectors

CSS selectors allow you to target specific HTML elements for styling. There are various types of selectors, including:

Element selectors: Select elements based on their tag name (e.g., p, h1, div).

ID selectors: Select elements with a specific ID attribute (e.g., #myElement).

Class selectors: Select elements with a specific class attribute (e.g., .myClass).

CSS Frameworks

CSS frameworks like Bootstrap and Foundation provide pre-built CSS rules and components that can accelerate your web development process. These frameworks offer responsive grid systems, pre-styled elements, and JavaScript plugins for creating interactive features.

Practice Time!

Experiment with different CSS properties and selectors. Style your HTML documents with various colors, fonts, and layouts. Explore online resources and tutorials to learn more about CSS and its vast capabilities. As you delve deeper into CSS, you'll unlock the power to create visually stunning and engaging web experiences.

Mission: Style one of their previous mission webpages with CSS to change its appearance and layout.

Solution:

```html
<!DOCTYPE html>
<html>
<head>
  <title>My Top 10</title>
  <style>
    body {
      font-family: sans-serif;
    }
    ol {
      list-style-type: upper-roman;
    }
  </style>
</head>
<body>
  <h1>My Top 10 Favorite Things</h1>
  <ol>
    <li>Pizza</li>
    <li>Coding</li>
    <li>Reading</li>
    <li>Hiking</li>
    <li>Music</li>
    <li>Movies</li>
    <li>Traveling</li>
    <li>Coffee</li>
    <li>Friends</li>
    <li>Family</li>
  </ol>
</body>
</html>
```

Webpage:

My Top 10 Favorite Things

  I. Pizza
  II. Coding
  III. Reading
  IV. Hiking
  V. Music
  VI. Movies
  VII. Traveling
 VIII. Coffee
  IX. Friends
  X. Family

Diving Deeper: HTML Attributes and Entities

While HTML elements provide the basic building blocks of webpages, attributes add further layers of meaning and functionality. Think of attributes as modifiers that provide additional information about an element. This chapter delves deeper into the world of HTML attributes, exploring their purpose, syntax, and common use cases. We'll also touch upon HTML entities, special characters that allow you to display symbols and characters that are not readily available on your keyboard.

Understanding HTML Attributes

Attributes are always specified within the opening tag of an element. They consist of a name and a value, separated by an equal's sign. The value is typically enclosed in quotation marks.

Here's the general syntax:

```
C: > Users > Biswajit > Desktop > index.html > html > body > elementName
1   <!DOCTYPE html>
2   <html>
3   <head>
4     <title>My News Article</title>
5   </head>
6   <body>
7       <elementName attributeName="attributeValue">...</elementName>
8   </body>
9   </html>
```

For example:

```
C: > Users > Biswajit > Desktop > index.html > html > body > img
1   <!DOCTYPE html>
2   <html>
3   <head>
4     <title>My News Article</title>
5   </head>
6   <body>
7       <img src="image.jpg" alt="A beautiful landscape">
8   </body>
9   </html>
```

In this code, src and alt are attributes of the <img> element. The src attribute specifies the image source, and the alt attribute provides alternative text.

Common HTML Attributes

HTML offers a wide array of attributes, each serving a specific purpose. Here are some commonly used attributes:

- src: Specifies the source URL for images, audio, and video files.

- alt: Provides alternative text for images.

- href: Specifies the destination URL for hyperlinks.

- class: Assigns one or more class names to an element for styling and scripting purposes.

- id: Assigns a unique ID to an element.

- style: Applies inline CSS styles to an element.

- title: Provides additional information about an element, often displayed as a tooltip.
  width and height: Specify the dimensions of an element.

- disabled: Disables a form control.

Global Attributes

Some attributes can be used with any HTML element. These are called global attributes. Some common global attributes include:

- class

- id

- style

- title

- lang (specifies the language of the element's content)

- data-* (used to store custom data)

HTML Entities

HTML entities are special characters that are represented by an ampersand (&) followed by a name or a number, and a semicolon (;). They allow you to display characters that are not readily available on your keyboard or that have special meaning in HTML.

Here are some common HTML entities:

- <: Less than symbol (<)

- >: Greater than symbol (>)

- &: Ampersand (&)

- : Non-breaking space

- ©: Copyright symbol (©)

- ®: Registered trademark symbol (®)

Using Entities

Entities are particularly useful when you need to display characters that have special meaning in HTML. For example, if you want to display the less than symbol (<) literally, you need to use the entity < instead of typing < directly, as the browser might interpret it as the beginning of an HTML tag.

Practice Time!

Explore different HTML attributes and experiment with their values. Use global attributes to add metadata and functionality to your elements. Familiarize yourself with common HTML entities and practice using them to display special characters. By mastering attributes and entities, you'll gain finer control over your HTML documents and be able to create more complex and feature-rich webpages.

Mission: Create a webpage with formatted text using various attributes and entities, like displaying quotes, copyright symbols, and special characters.

Solution:

```html
<!DOCTYPE html>
<html>
<head>
    <title>Attributes and Entities</title>
</head>
<body>
    <p>This is a paragraph with a <span style="color: blue;">blue</span> word.</p>
    <p>He said, &ldquo;Hello world!&rdquo;</p>
    <p>This website is &copy; 2024 My Company.</p>
    <p>The price is &euro;10.</p>
</body>
</html>
```

Webpage:

This is a paragraph with a blue word.

He said, "Hello world!"

This website is © 2024 My Company.

The price is €10.

Building Blocks: Exploring HTML5 Layout Elements

HTML5 introduced a set of semantic elements specifically designed to define different parts of a webpage. These elements provide structural clarity, improve accessibility, and enhance SEO by clearly identifying the purpose of various sections within a webpage. This chapter explores these essential HTML5 layout elements, empowering you to create well-structured and meaningful webpages.

<header>: Defining the Page Header

The <header> element represents the introductory content of a webpage or a section within a page. It typically contains elements like the site logo, navigation menu, search bar, and introductory text.

```
index.html ×

C: > Users > Biswajit > Desktop > index.html > html > head > title
1    <!DOCTYPE html>
2    <html>
3    <head>
4        <title>HTML5</title>
5    </head>
6    <body>
7        <header>
8            <h1>Welcome to My Website</h1>
9            <nav>
10               <ul>
11                   <li><a href="#">Home</a></li>
12                   <li><a href="#">About</a></li>
13                   <li><a href="#">Contact</a></li>
14               </ul>
15           </nav>
16       </header>>
17   </body>
18   </html>
```

← → C ⓘ File C:/Users/Biswajit/Desktop/index.html

Welcome to My Website

- Home
- About
- Contact

<nav>: Marking Up Navigation Links

The <nav> element defines a section of navigation links, typically used for main menus, tables of contents, or other sets of links that aid in site navigation.

```
index.html ×

C: > Users > Biswajit > Desktop > index.html > html > body > nav
1    <!DOCTYPE html>
2    <html>
3      <head>
4        <title>HTML5</title>
5      </head>
6      <body>
7        <nav>
8          <ul>
9            <li><a href="#">Products</a></li>
10           <li><a href="#">Services</a></li>
11           <li><a href="#">Support</a></li>
12         </ul>
13        </nav>
14      </body>
15    </html>
16
```

<main>: Identifying the Main Content

The <main> element specifies the main content area of a webpage. It should contain the primary content that the page is about, excluding content that is repeated across multiple pages, such as sidebars or navigation menus.

```
index.html ×

C: > Users > Biswajit > Desktop > index.html > html > body > main
1    <!DOCTYPE html>
2    <html>
3      <head>
4        <title>HTML5</title>
5      </head>
6      <body>
7        <main>
8          <article>
9            <h2>Article Title</h2>
10           <p>This is the main content of the article.</p>
11          </article>
12        </main>
13      </body>
14    </html>
15
```

<article>: Encapsulating Independent Content

The <article> element represents a self-contained composition in a document, page, application, or site. It is typically used for blog posts, news articles, forum posts, or any other independent piece of content.

```html
index.html ×
C: > Users > Biswajit > Desktop > index.html > html > body > article
1  <!DOCTYPE html>
2  <html>
3    <head>
4      <title>HTML5</title>
5    </head>
6    <body>
7      <article>
8          <h2>Article Title</h2>
9          <p>This is the content of the article.</p>
10     </article>
11   </body>
12 </html>
13
```

<aside>: Defining Tangential Content

The <aside> element defines content that is tangentially related to the main content of the document. It is often used for sidebars, pull quotes, or advertising.

```html
index.html ×
C: > Users > Biswajit > Desktop > index.html > html > body > aside
1  <!DOCTYPE html>
2  <html>
3    <head>
4      <title>HTML5</title>
5    </head>
6    <body>
7      <aside>
8          <h3>Related Articles</h3>
9          <ul>
10             <li><a href="#">Article 1</a></li>
11             <li><a href="#">Article 2</a></li>
12         </ul>
13     </aside>
14   </body>
15 </html>
16
```

\<footer>: Marking Up the Page Footer

The \<footer> element defines the footer of a webpage or a section. It typically contains information like copyright notices, contact details, or links to related pages.

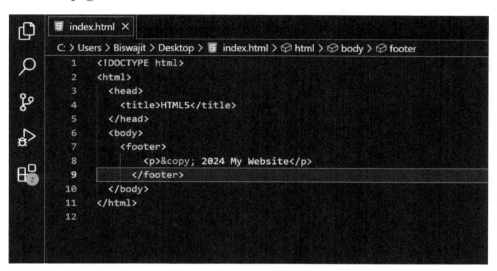

```
     index.html ×

C: > Users > Biswajit > Desktop >    index.html >    html >    body >    footer
1    <!DOCTYPE html>
2    <html>
3      <head>
4        <title>HTML5</title>
5      </head>
6      <body>
7        <footer>
8          <p>&copy; 2024 My Website</p>
9        </footer>
10     </body>
11   </html>
12
```

\<section>: Grouping Thematic Content

The \<section> element defines a generic section of a document or application. It is used to group content that shares a common theme or purpose.

```
     index.html ×

C: > Users > Biswajit > Desktop >    index.html > ...
1    <!DOCTYPE html>
2    <html>
3      <head>
4        <title>HTML5</title>
5      </head>
6      <body>
7        <section>
8          <h2>Section Title</h2>
9          <p>This is the content of the section.</p>
10       </section>
11     </body>
12   </html>
13
```

Combining Layout Elements

These HTML5 layout elements can be combined to create complex and well-structured webpages. For example, a webpage might have a <header> with a <nav> inside, a <main> containing multiple <article> elements, and an <aside> for related content, all followed by a <footer>.

Practice Time!

Analyse the structure of different websites and identify how HTML5 layout elements are used. Practice creating your own webpages using these elements to define the different sections and content types. By mastering these building blocks, you can create semantically rich and well-organized webpages that are accessible, maintainable, and SEO-friendly.

Mission: Refactor a previous mission's webpage using these elements to demonstrate their practical application.

Solution:

```html
index.html ×

C: > Users > Biswajit > Desktop > 🖥 index.html > ...
1    <!DOCTYPE html>
2  ∨ <html>
3  ∨   <head>
4        <title>The Amazing Widget</title>
5      </head>
6  ∨   <body>
7  ∨     <header>
8          <h1>The Amazing Widget</h1>
9        </header>
10       <main></main>
11     </body>
12 </html>
13
```

Congratulations!

You've reached the end of this journey through the fundamentals of HTML. You've learned the essential building blocks of webpages, from basic structure and text formatting to embedding multimedia and creating interactive forms. You've even had a glimpse into the world of styling with CSS.

But this is just the beginning. The world of web development is vast and ever-evolving. There's always something new to learn, a new skill to master, a new challenge to conquer.

Keep Learning, Keep Building

Embrace the journey. Explore new technologies, experiment with different techniques, and never stop learning. Build your own websites, contribute to open-source projects, and share your knowledge with others.

Resources for Your Journey

- **MDN Web Docs:** https://developer.mozilla.org/en-US/docs/Web/HTML
- W3Schools: https://www.w3schools.com/html/
- Codecademy: https://www.codecademy.com/
- freeCodeCamp: https://www.freecodecamp.org/

Thank You

Thank you for joining us on this adventure into the world of HTML. We hope this book has sparked your passion for web development and equipped you with the foundational knowledge to build your own amazing websites.

Now go forth and create!

Tips and Tricks for VS Code

Visual Studio Code (VS Code) is a powerful code editor that can significantly boost your productivity and streamline your web development workflow. Here are some tips and tricks to help you get the most out of VS Code:

- Command Palette Mastery: The Command Palette is your gateway to VS Code's extensive functionality. Access it with Ctrl+Shift+P (Windows) or Cmd+Shift+P (macOS) and explore the myriads of commands available.

- Emmet Abbreviations: Emmet is a built-in feature that allows you to write HTML and CSS code quickly using abbreviations. For example, typing! and pressing Tab will generate a basic HTML5 template.

- Extensions Galore: Explore the vast library of extensions in the VS Code Marketplace. These extensions can add support for new languages, frameworks, and tools, enhancing your coding experience.

- Keyboard Shortcuts: Learn and utilize keyboard shortcuts for common actions like formatting code, navigating between files, and commenting/uncommenting code. Integrated Terminal: Leverage the

- integrated terminal to run commands, manage version control, and interact with your project without leaving VS Code. Multi-Cursor Editing: Edit multiple lines

- simultaneously by holding Alt (Windows) or Option (macOS) and clicking in different locations.

- Zen Mode: Minimize distractions and focus on your code by entering Zen Mode (View -> Appearance -> Toggle Zen Mode).

- Code Snippets: Create and use code snippets to quickly insert frequently used blocks of code.

- Live Server: The Live Server extension allows you to see your webpage updates in real-time as you save your code.

- Debugging Tools: Utilize VS Code's debugging tools to identify and fix errors in your code.

By incorporating these tips and tricks into your workflow, you can unlock the full potential of VS Code and become a more efficient and productive web developer.

Got Questions?

We're here to help! If you have any questions, doubts, or encounter any roadblocks while exploring the world of HTML, feel free to reach out. You can contact the author directly at aritradebnath1@gmail.com.

www.ingramcontent.com/pod-product-compliance
Lightning Source LLC
LaVergne TN
LVHW080119070326
832902LV00015B/2671